HOW TO DRAW
CATHEDRALS
AND CHURCHES

Mark Bergin

BOOK HOUSE

Published in Great Britain in MMXVIII by
Book House, an imprint of
The Salariya Book Company Ltd
25 Marlborough Place, Brighton BN1 1UB
www.salariya.com

ISBN: 978-1-912006-31-1

1 3 5 7 9 8 6 4 2

A CIP catalogue record for this book is available
from the British Library.

Printed and bound in China.

Author: **Mark Bergin** was born in Hastings
in 1961. He studied at Eastbourne College of Art
and has specialised in historical reconstructions as
well as aviation and maritime subjects since 1983.
He lives in Bexhill-on-Sea with his wife and three
children.

Editor: Nick Pierce

Visit
www.salariya.com
for our online catalogue and
free fun stuff.

PAPER FROM
SUSTAINABLE
FORESTS

Contents

Making a start

Learning to draw is about looking and seeing. Keep practising and get to know your subject. Use a sketchbook to make quick drawings. Start by doodling, and experiment with shapes and patterns. There are many ways to draw, and this book shows only some of them. Visit cathedrals and churches, look at artists' drawings, see how friends draw, but above all, find your own way.

Rosslyn Chapel carvings

Dry Drayton Methodist Church, Cambridgeshire

Salzburg Cathedral

Rosslyn Chapel carvings

4

All Saint's Church in
Herstmonceux, Sussex

Glasgow Cathedral

Practise drawing on site or use
photographs as a reference. Build
up your drawings using very
simple shapes. Add detail as the
drawing progresses.

Drawing materials

Try using different types of drawing paper and materials. Experiment with charcoal, wax crayons and pastels. All pens, from felt–tips to ballpoints, will make interesting marks — or try drawing with pen and ink on wet paper.

Ink silhouette

Remember, the best equipment and materials will not necessarily make the best drawing — only practice will!

Pencil drawings can include a vast amount of detail and tone. Try experimenting with different grades of pencil to get a range of light and shade effects in your drawing.

Pencil

Colouring pencils and **felt—tip pens** are simple to use, and experimenting with them will result in drawings that are vibrant and intriguing.

Colouring pencils

Ink

Lines drawn in **ink** cannot be erased, so keep your ink drawings sketchy and less rigid. Don't worry about mistakes, as these lines can be lost in the drawing as it develops.

Adding light and shade to a drawing with an ink pen can be tricky. Use solid ink for the very darkest areas and cross—hatching for less dark tones. Use hatching for midtones, and leave the white of the paper for the lightest areas.

Crosshatching is the use of straight lines that criss—cross each other. **Hatching** is when short parallel lines are used to create tone.

7

Perspective

If you look at anything from different viewpoints, you will see that the part that is closest to you looks larger, and the part furthest away from you looks smaller. Drawing in perspective is a way of creating a feeling of space — of showing three dimensions on a flat surface.

The vanishing point (V.P.) is the place in a perspective drawing where parallel lines appear to meet. The position of the vanishing point depends on the viewer's eye level.

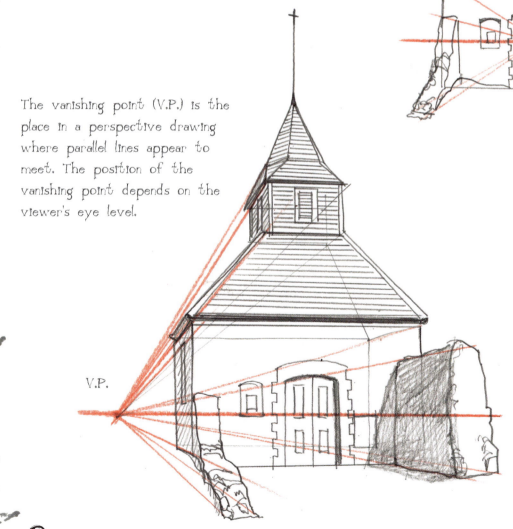

V.P.

8

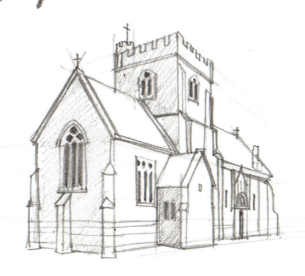

Two-point perspective uses two vanishing points: one for lines running along the length of the subject, and one on the opposite side for lines running across the width of the subject.

V.P.   V.P.

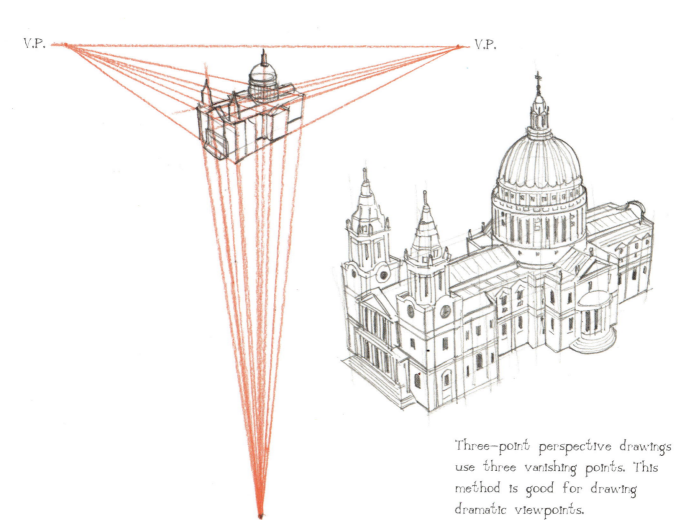

Three-point perspective drawings use three vanishing points. This method is good for drawing dramatic viewpoints.

9

How to use photos

Drawing from photographs is a useful way to study shape and proportion. Copying a photograph is a good way to start. It's also much easier than trying to draw on site where you have to contend with the weather and nosy passers-by!

First choose a good, clear photograph to trace. Then draw a grid of squares over the tracing (as shown).

Now lightly draw a grid of the same proportions onto your drawing paper. To increase the grid size for a longer drawing, simply enlarge the scale of the grid squares. Copy the shapes within each square of the tracing paper onto your drawing—paper grid.

Once the general shape is complete, start adding more detail to your drawing. Always refer back to the grid for accuracy. To add form to your drawing, see where the light falls on your subject, and add shadows to the parts that face away from the light source.

11

St Martin's Church

This church in Bladon in Oxfordshire, England, is the burial place of British prime minister, Winston Churchill. The first church on this site was probably built in the 11th or 12th centuries. Extensive restorations and additions to the medieval church were undertaken in the late 19th century.

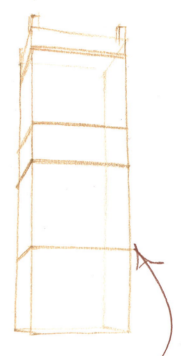

Start by sketching in a tall rectangular shape for the church tower.

Now sketch in the outline of the nave and the entranceway. Add windows to the tower and the church door.

12

Add further details: windows in the nave, various crucifixes adorning the structure and a weather vane on top of the tower.

Start sketching in the surrounding tree line and pathways.

Draw in the clockface and the gravestones, monuments and trees in the surrounding area. Add shading for darker areas of colour and to show the direction of the light. Use scribbly lines for added texture.

Erase all unwanted construction lines.

13

Iona Abbey

This Benedictine abbey is located on the Isle of Iona in Argyll, Scotland. It is believed that the world-famous Book of Kells, an illuminated manuscript of the Gospels, was originally made here before its eventual journey to Ireland.

Start by drawing the outline of the nave using simple rectangle and cube shapes.

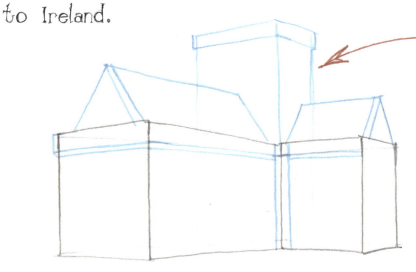

Add the roof of the nave and draw in the tower.

Now draw in the outline of the monastic buildings alongside the church of the abbey.

Start to position the basic
features, such as the windows
and doorways.

Sketch all remaining details. Add a crucifix
to the top of the tower and another to
the nave gable. Draw in the base line and
pathways in the vicinity.

Add all finishing touches. Use scribbled or hatched
lines to create the effect of the slate roof. Add
shading to the picture to show the direction of
the light, and add texture to the stonework.

Erase all unwanted construction lines.

15

Canterbury Cathedral

Mother Church of the Anglican Communion, Canterbury Cathedral in Kent, England is also the seat of the Archbishop of Canterbury. It is a World Heritage Site and has been described as 'England in stone' because of its connection to many significant events in English history.

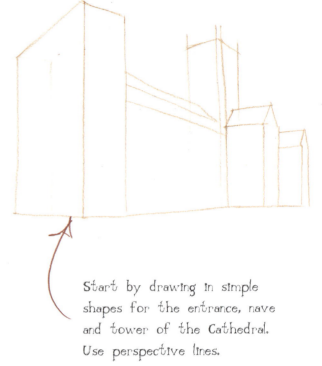

Start by drawing in simple shapes for the entrance, nave and tower of the Cathedral. Use perspective lines.

Start adding some of the more decorative features to the facade and draw in the Cathedral tower.

Add more detail. Carefully position all doorways and windows, and draw in the line of flying buttresses along the side wall.

Slowly build up all the finer details to complete your drawing. Add shading to indicate the direction of the light and to add textual interest.

Erase all unwanted construction lines.

17

Whitby Abbey

The ruins of this Benedictine abbey are located in Whitby in North Yorkshire, England. They overlook the North Sea and are a popular destination for tourists in the area. The ruins famously feature in Bram Stoker's novel, *Dracula*, serving as the site where the monster comes ashore in the form of a large black dog.

Start by drawing simple shapes for the front and side walls of the nave of the abbey.

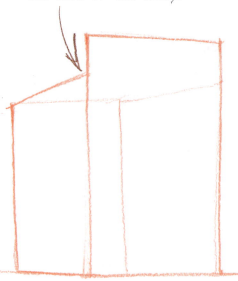

Add spires to the facade of the abbey and draw in the smaller ruins beside it.

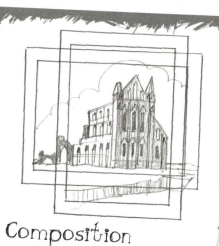

Composition

Composition is the arrangement of a picture, or the various parts of it, on the paper. Does your drawing look better in an upright (portrait) format or in a horizontal (landscape) format?

Now start to draw in the many window spaces and archways of the ruins. Roughly sketch in the area in front of the abbey.

Add all final details, including the reflection of the ruins in the nearby water. Draw in the posts at the side and add clouds to create atmosphere. Use shading to indicate the direction of light and very dark shading within the ruined shell to emphasise its emptiness.

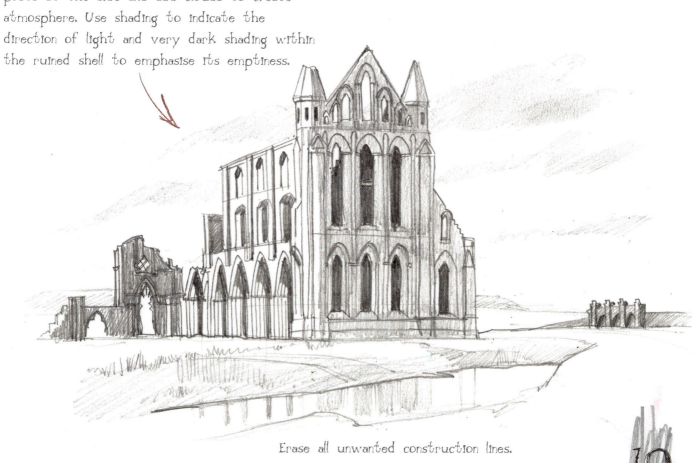

Erase all unwanted construction lines.

19

Liverpool Metropolitan Cathedral

This is the largest Catholic cathedral in England. The designer of the current cathedral was architect Sir Frederick Gibberd, who won the competition held in 1960 to find a design for a new cathedral on this site. The completed cathedral was consecrated on 14 May, 1967.

Start by drawing a wide triangle. Add a cylindrical shape to its apex to create the outline of the cathedral's shape.

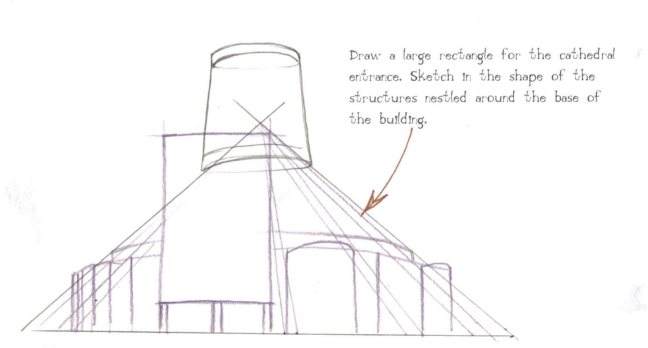

Draw a large rectangle for the cathedral entrance. Sketch in the shape of the structures nestled around the base of the building.

Now draw in the spires of the upper section of the tower. Start adding further details: the decorative crucifix over the cathedral entrance and the bells above. Draw in the structural detail of the lower tower.

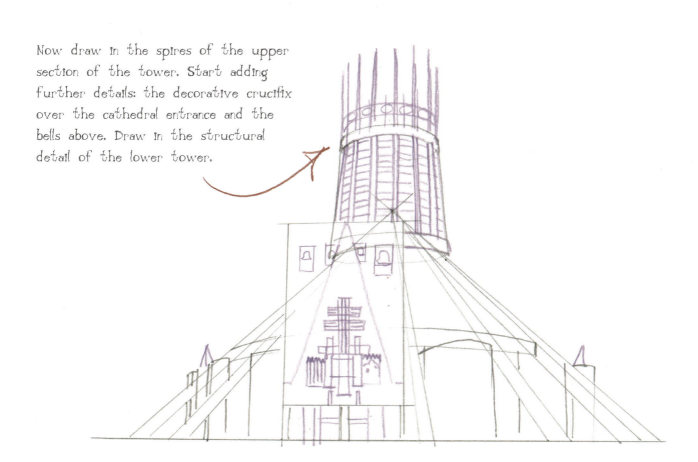

Add all final details. Sketch in some trees and add clouds to the sky. Use shading to show the direction of light and add any textural details to the cathedral.

Erase all unwanted construction lines.

St Patrick's Cathedral

This Church of Ireland cathedral is located in the city of Armagh, the ecclesiastical capital of Ireland. It sits on a hill called the Ard Macha, from which the city derives its name.

Start by drawing in the nave of the cathedral between two tall rectangular towers.

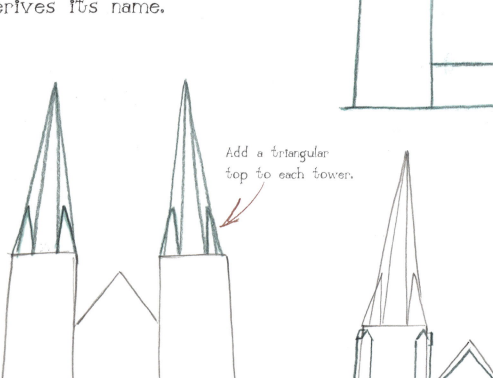

Add a triangular top to each tower.

Sketch in the shorter wings of the cathedral either side of the towers.

Now you can begin to add details to the facade of the cathedral. Carefully position its windows, doorways and crucifixes. Draw in the large stained glass window in the centre.

Add shading to indicate the direction of the light. Draw in the stairs in the foreground that lead up to the cathedral site. Add clouds and birds flying by to create added interest.

Erase all unwanted construction lines.

St Giles' Cathedral

The City Church of Edinburgh is famous for its crown steeple. It was founded in 1124 AD, but the original structure was burned down by an invading English army in 1322. The cathedral was subsequently rebuilt in a Gothic style that has largely been preserved until the present day.

Start by drawing a rectangular box shape for the cathedral nave.

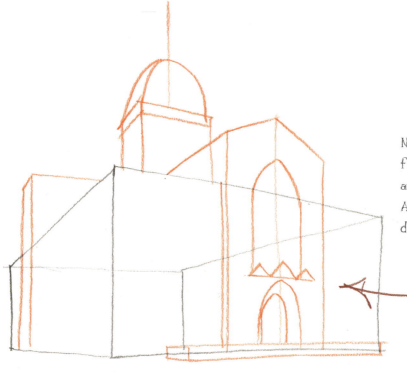

Now draw in the shape of the front facade, including its doorway and large stained glass window above. Add the steeple tower and the domed shape of the crown.

Continue adding all the architectural details.
Carefully position and draw in its many ornate
windows. Sketch in the shape of the spiked
spars of the crown steeple.

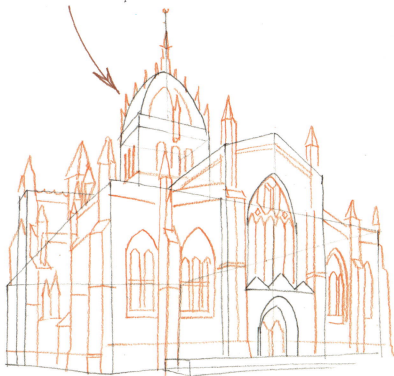

Use A Mirror

It's worth looking at your
drawing in a mirror. Seeing
it in reverse often helps
you to spot mistakes.

Add all finishing details, including the
statue of Walter Scott in front of
the cathedral. Draw in people walking
around it to give a sense of scale.
Add shading to indicate the direction
of light and the dark interior of
the cathedral.

Erase all unwanted construction lines.

Rosslyn Chapel

Founded in 1446 AD, this chapel is located in Midlothian, Scotland. It has become famous in recent years for its legendary connections with the Knights Templar. It also featured in the bestselling book *The Da Vinci Code* by Dan Brown, and its film adaptation.

Start by drawing in the rectangular planes of the chapel (as shown).

Now start to add the many spiked pillars situated along the outside walls of the chapel nave.

Continue adding more details. Draw
in all windows, the entrance portal
and the decorative carvings on
the facade.

Sketch in the grass and the
pathway leading to the Chapel.
Add shading to indicate the
direction of the light and the
dark shadowed interior.

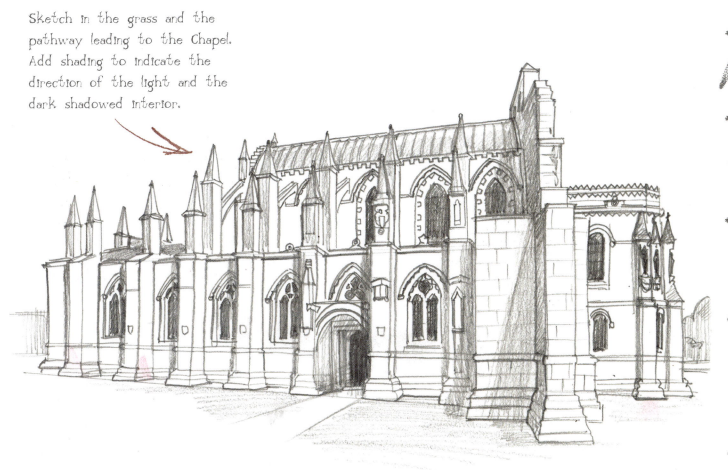

Erase all unwanted construction lines.

27

Westminster Abbey

Westminster Abbey has been the coronation church since 1066. It is the final resting place of many famous people, including seventeen monarchs, Charles Darwin, Isaac Newton, Charles Dickens and William Shakespeare. The most recent parts of the building are the West Towers, completed to a design by famous architect, Nicholas Hawksmoor in 1745 AD.

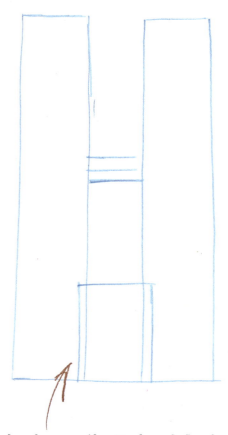

Start by drawing the H-shaped facade created by the two towers and the abbey nave. Add the entrance.

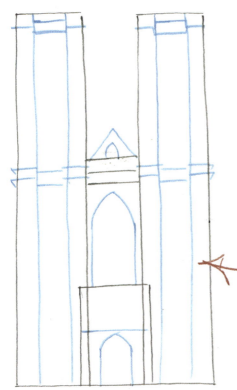

Draw in the entrance doorway, the roof of the nave and the shape of the huge stained glass window above the entrance.

Negative space

Look at the negative space around your drawing, too. This can alert you to any problem areas within the drawing.

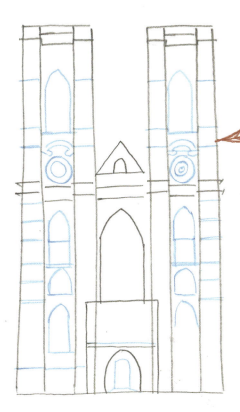

Start adding more details. Carefully position all windows and carved sections on the facade. Add the clockface to the left—hand tower.

Add more detail to the carved decorative facade. Draw in the spires and pole flag. Sketch in the lower part of the building that runs alongside it.

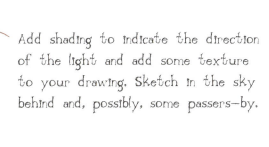

Add shading to indicate the direction of the light and add some texture to your drawing. Sketch in the sky behind and, possibly, some passers—by.

Erase all unwanted construction lines.

29

St Paul's Cathedral

The cathedral was founded in 604 AD. The old building burned down during the Great Fire of London in 1666. It was rebuilt to a grand new design by one of England's greatest architects, Sir Christopher Wren.

Start by drawing a rectangular box shape for the body of the cathedral. Add a cylindrical shape for the base of its dome.

Start building up the shape of the cathedral. Draw in the side entrance. Add the dome with its spire on top and the smaller tower at the far end.

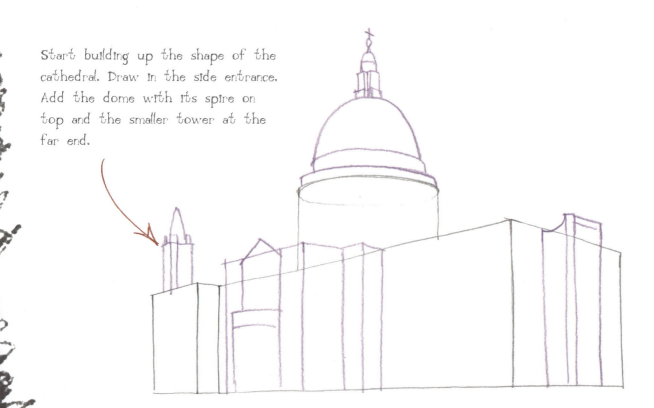

Now start adding more detail. Draw
in the two levels of windows that
surround the cathedral and add columns
around the dome.

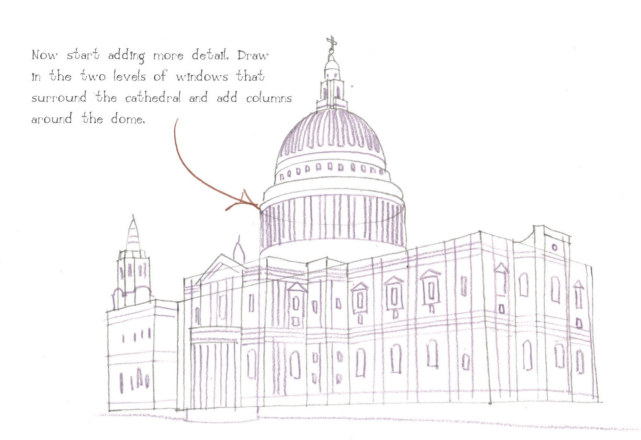

Add shading to indicate the direction
of the light and the darkened interior.
Add textural interest to your
drawing. Sketch in some clouds behind
or even some birds or a plane to
complete the scene.

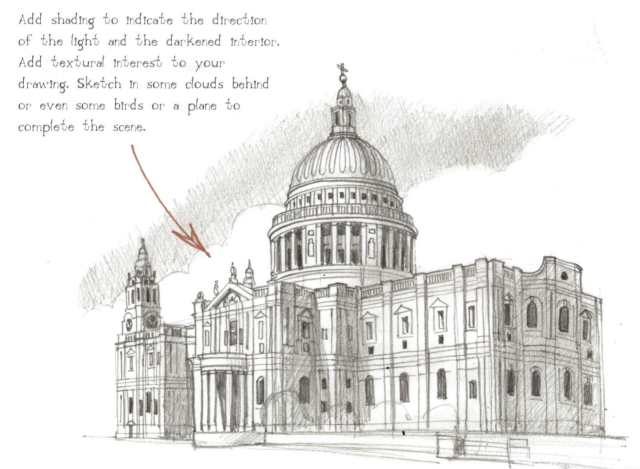

Erase all unwanted construction lines.

31

Glossary

Composition The arrangement of the parts of a picture on the drawing paper.

Construction lines Guidelines used in the early stages of a drawing; they may be erased later.

Cross-hatching The use of criss-crossed lines to indicate dense shade in a drawing.

Hatching The use of parallel lines to indicate light shade in a drawing.

Negative space The empty space between the parts of a drawing, often an important part of the composition.

Perspective A method of drawing in which near objects are shown larger than faraway objects to give an impression of depth.

Silhouette A drawing that shows only a flat dark shape, like a shadow.

Index